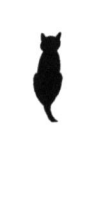

A MIX OF A MYSTERY

Cats with Their Own Point of View

Poems & Watercolors

by

Susan Gail Lawrence

COPYRIGHT

A Mix of a Mystery
Cats with Their Own Point of View
Poems and Watercolors by Susan Gail Lawrence

Books > Art > Poetry > Cats

ISBN-10:
1537134442
EAN-13
978-1537134444

CONTENTS

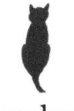

Introduction
Dedication

INTRODUCTION

This art and poetry book, *A Mix of a Mystery,* is a look at the way cats may think about things. It is filled with the mystery and love that cats bring us. If you have ever wondered what your family cat or neighborhood stray may be thinking at any given moment, this book offers some insight into their innermost thoughts. I hope that this book brings you closer to your cat, so that you can have a better understanding and communication of trust with him or her. The poems and artwork are designed to be a cozy companion to settle down with when you want to enjoy the mysterious world of cats.

DEDICATION

To my two Mikes, and to Collette who
helped to make this book possible

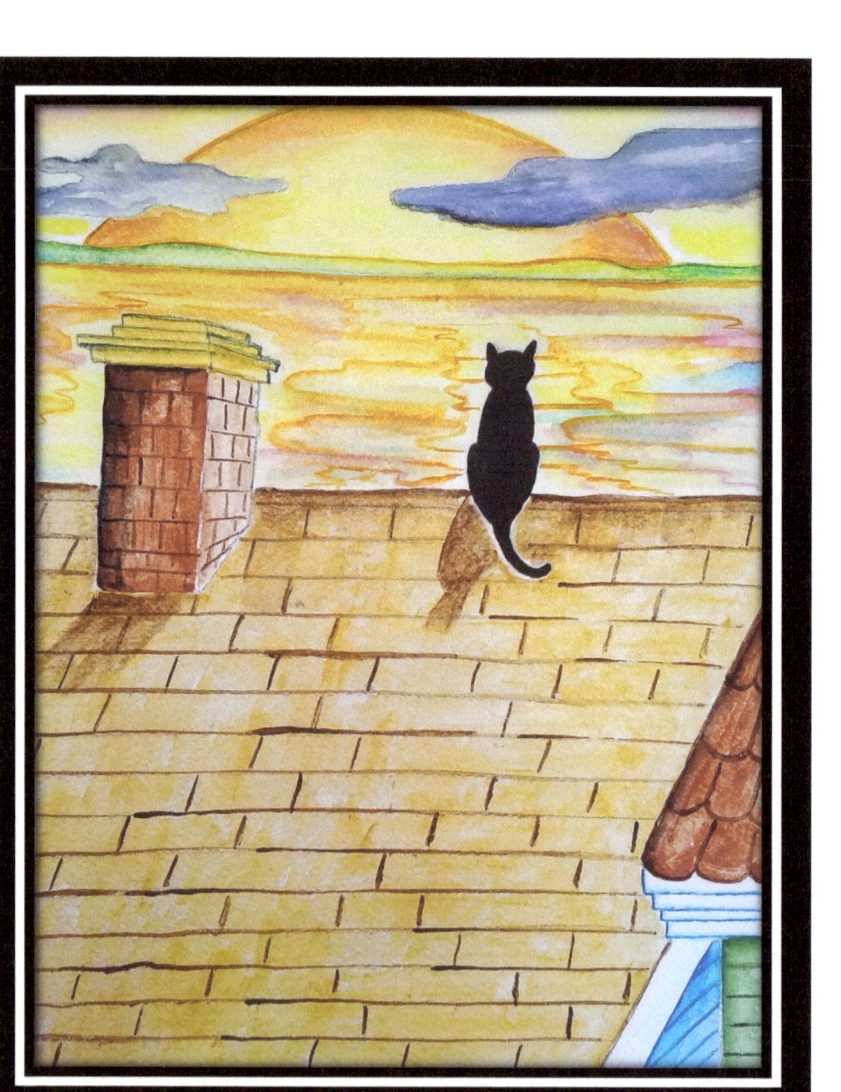

Enchanted Cat

When I sit high upon this
   roof of tar before this night
And watch the luminous setting sun
   with intuitive insight
I can see grey clouds cross by
   the radiant sky of mixed hues
As I go back over the magic of past
   lives I've gone through
And if this has to be the last of all
   these mysterious years
Where I must say goodbye to my
   family in quiet tears
I will remind them to love and to
   always be strong
Determined to live to a beat of a
   special enchanted song

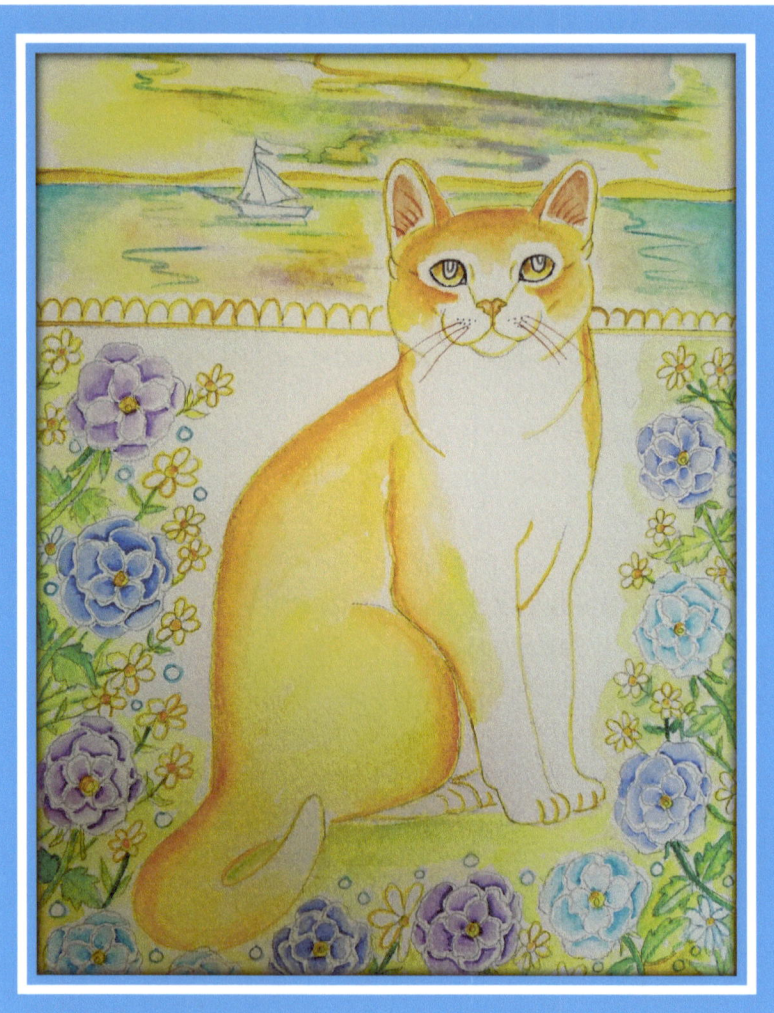

Enchanted Love

Sleeping on a quilt of stars
   and diamonds in design
I, a gold cat, dream about
   cats close in my mind
I'm near a sparkling river, I see
   flowers and green around
We are small felines like tigers
   running on a golden lit ground
I often think back to how good it was
   to be alongside of someone and run
When wide awake we remember the
   mystery, a cat's play, and the fun
But most important there was a
   dignified cat, mysterious and smart
She will always be remembered for
   her wisdom and kind heart
She reminded us to carry a song with us
   wherever we go
It's the enchanted love, this
   enchanted cat endeared us to know

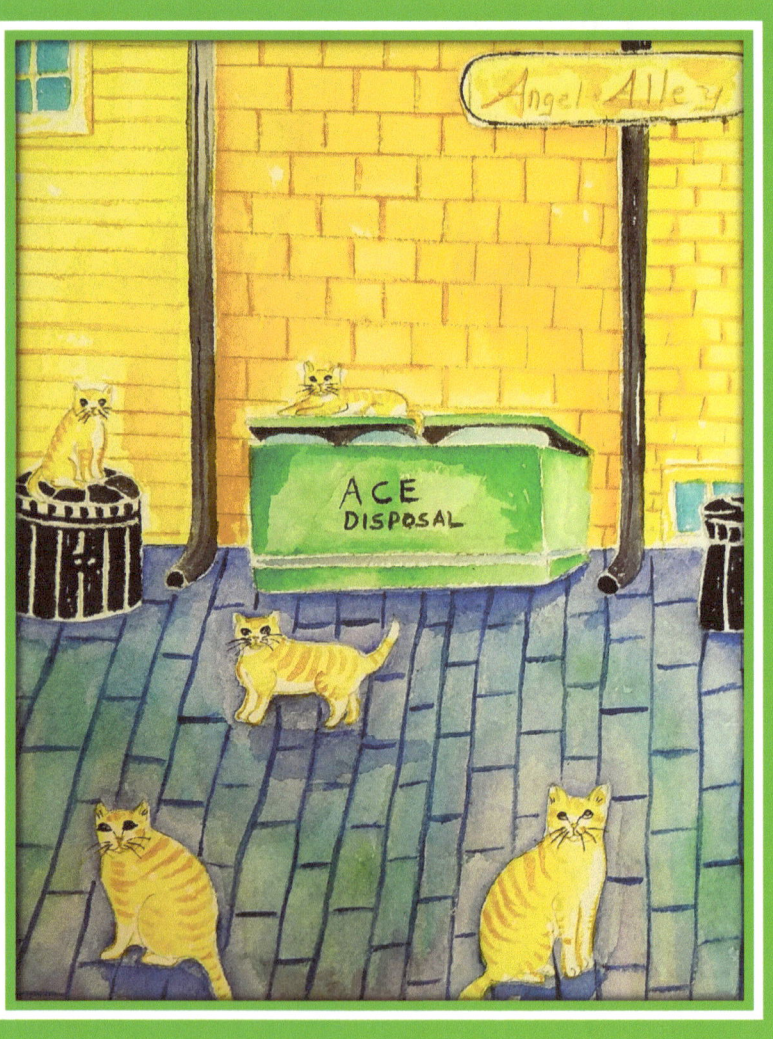

The Double

I was a cat who lived in a cottage
    down on Toffee Lane
As I peered into the mirror I saw an
    image of myself out in the rain
How could I find this feline who
    looked exactly like me
This cat was a mystery I had to find out
    about and see
And then in my yard, she was there again
    in the tall old oak
She said we were from Angel Alley, she
    was honest as she spoke
As we sat together she said the cats from
    our family were all moved across town
Suddenly this tree branch made a noisy
    squeak, we thought we should climb down
Then the limb gave way our weight was
    more than it could hold
Dangerously jumping we landed on our feet
    we knew the two of us could be bold
Now we have a true friendship
    we are siblings but with one less life to go
We want to spend the next eight
    remembering
The family of cats we scarcely got to know

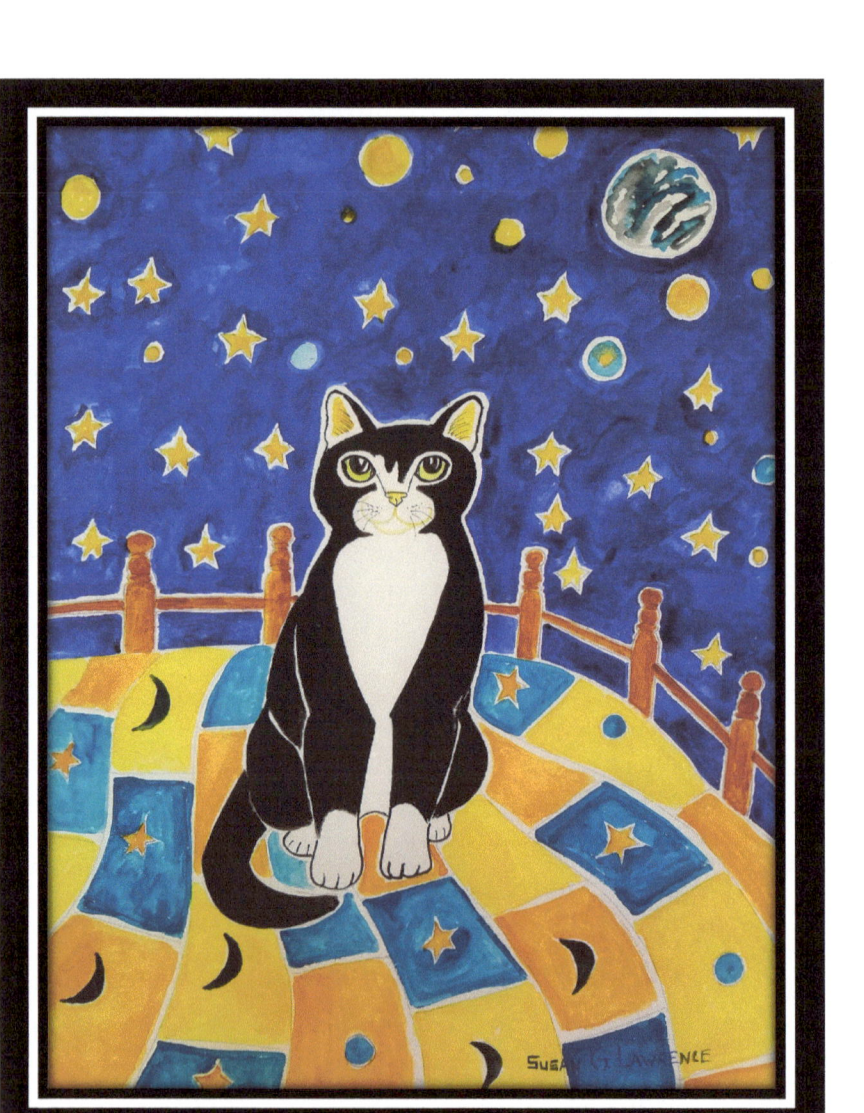

Venus

My name is Venus
   my eyes are green and bright
My black fur is shiny
   in the early light
I wasn't shy and had a very
   good true friend
She helped my world to be happy
   and my spirit to mend
We lived in a house together
   but sometimes I was far away
Our bond was very special
   'til the end of each day
Because I really came from
   another place beyond so far
I know it's where the essence of
   angelic little cats really are
So if you ever see a radiant sparkle
   from a planet in the night sky
There was a goddess who sent me to earth
   love is the reason why

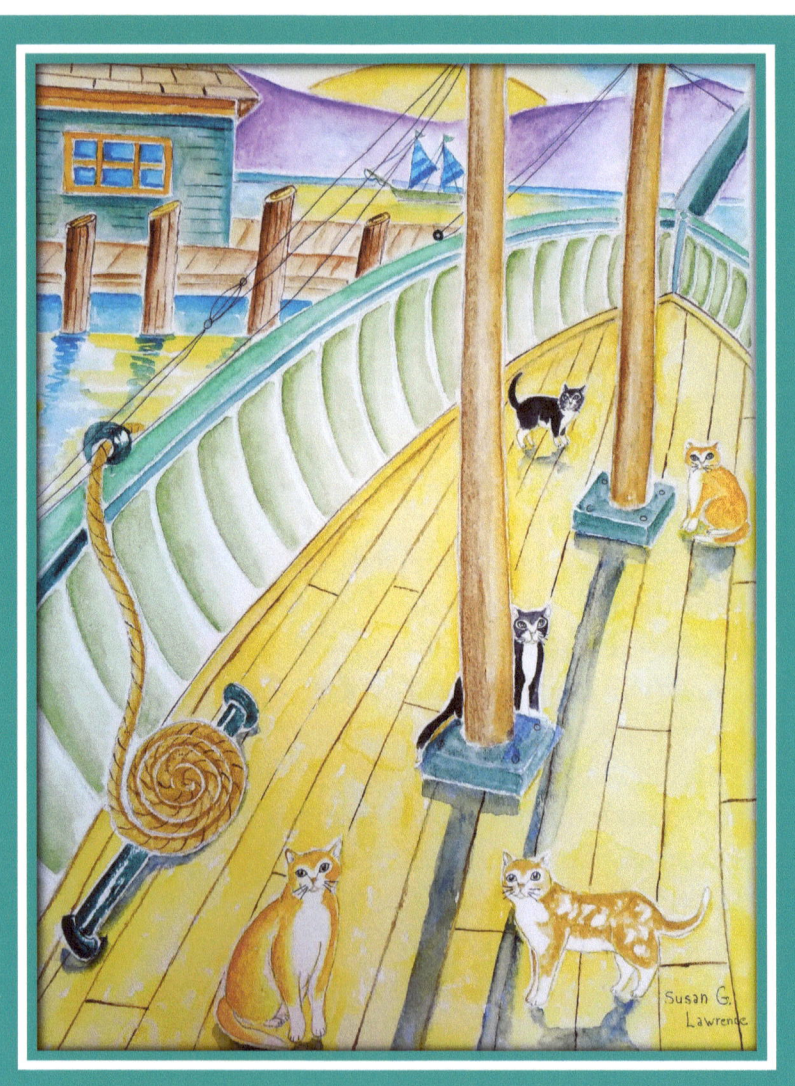

When We Were Aboard a Vessel

As the waves crashed and mists
   of salt water blew upon the deck
Our distended sails were headed for
   home, the cats kept everything in check
As we pulled into the village port
   and anchored at the bright dock
The seamen would have a day to rest
   to visit and to talk
We have been the cats that are
   here to work, numbering ten
We have helped chase rats around
   we could do better than the men
As the sailors knew without us
   their food stock would be lost
Their voyage would have been more
   difficult, their love for the sea star-crossed

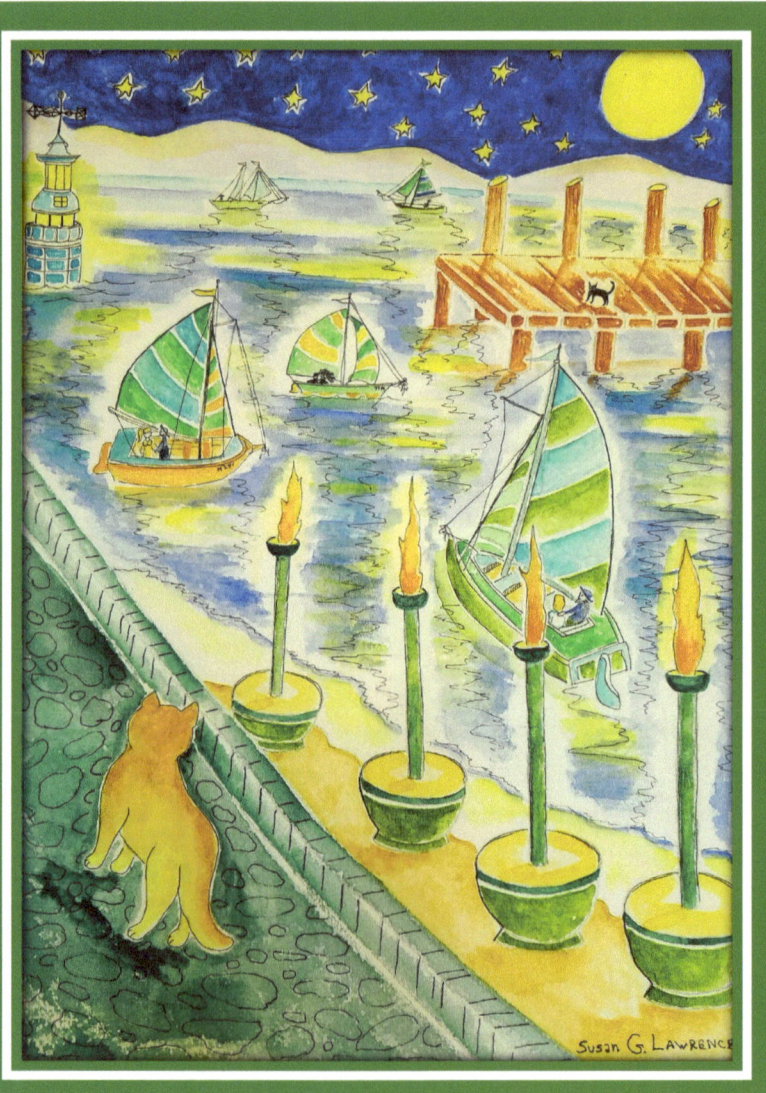

Over the Bridge

I'm walking over a stone bridge
   below me are fire and lights
There are sentimental people here
   it's a comforting sight
Under these twinkling stars I am
   hoping to wish on something too
That a special love will come my way
   a beginning of a life brand new
In this romantic place I want to
   dream in this mysterious glow
From beyond the boats, I see her
   a beautiful cat, I feel I know
Now she is the gypsy I fell in love
   with that night over the sea
There must have been an ancient captain
   out there who sent her to me

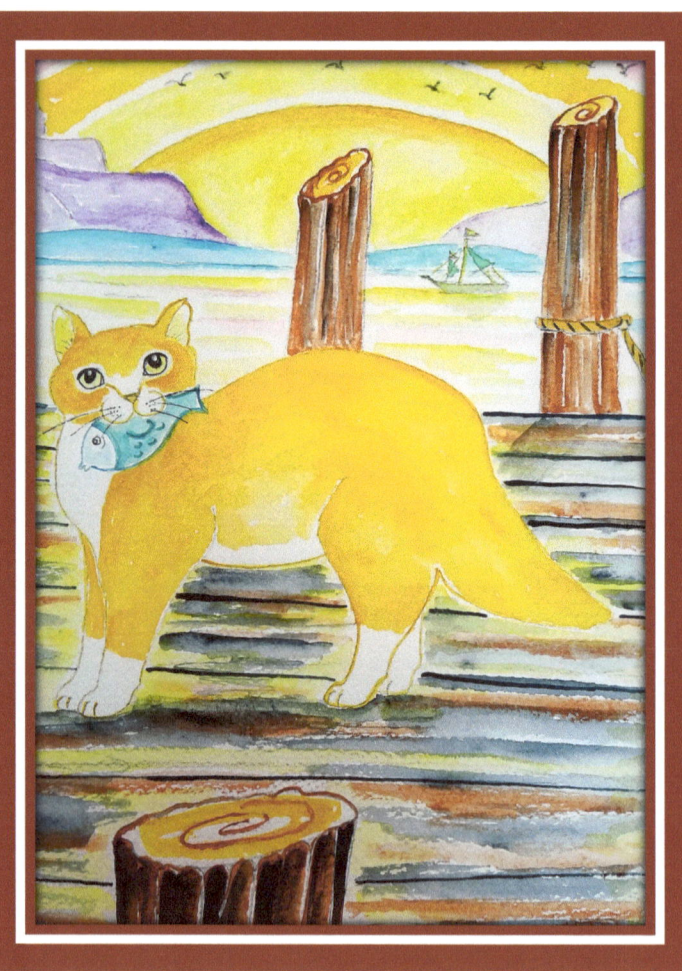

The Fishing Wharf

Smelling the fish as I
    walk along the boards
I've been a good cat and this
    can be my reward
The pigeons they walk close
    but then want to go astray
Maybe I can hide somewhere
    like a stowaway
But I can see a fish now
    that's fallen out of its net
Will I be able to snatch it
    all I can say is, you bet
Then away I run with a fish
    held in my teeth
As I heard in my head
    "with this fish I bequeath"

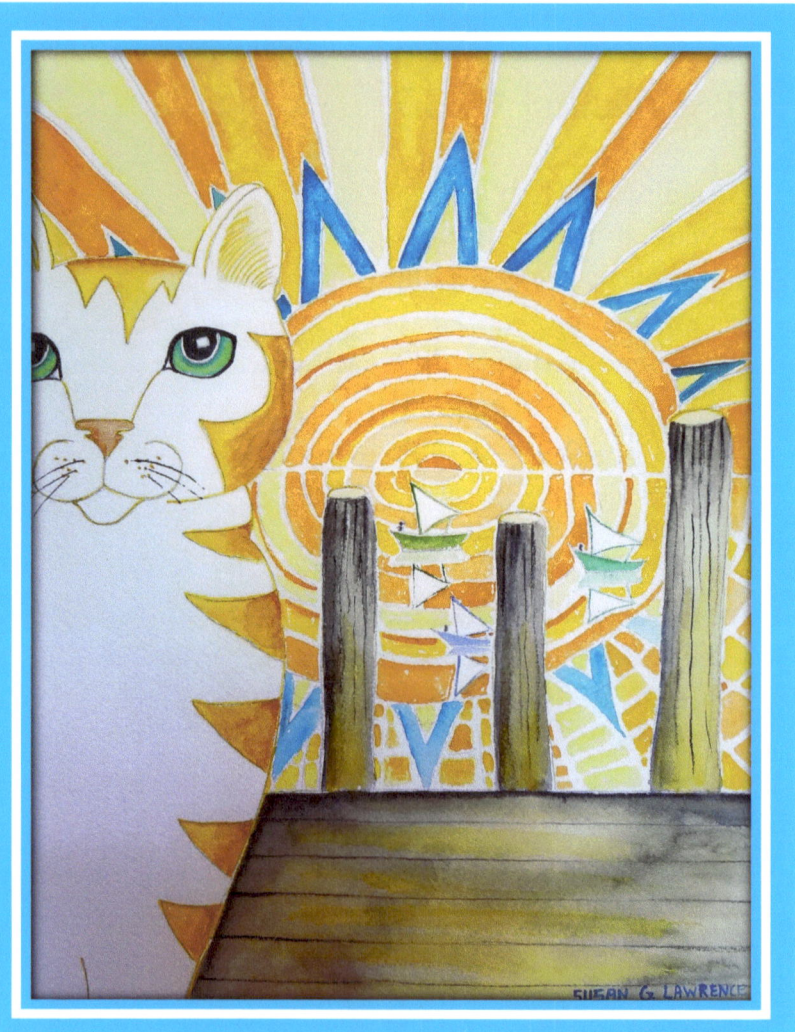

A Return to the Wharf

Yesterday I was lucky
   I ended up with a fish
So I came back to this wharf
   hoping or only to wish
That the net that was there before
   may reappear today
So that I might be able by tonight
   to have a dish of moray
It's only the morning
   I may have hours to wait
Now I see a boat pulling in
   with seafood top rate
So like a bandit, I slink by
   with a look of gloom
Then I seize a catch and fly
   down the dock with a zoom
There really is no secret or even
   an uncommon code
I have the eyes of a tiger
   for a drop-out, in a bounty ton load

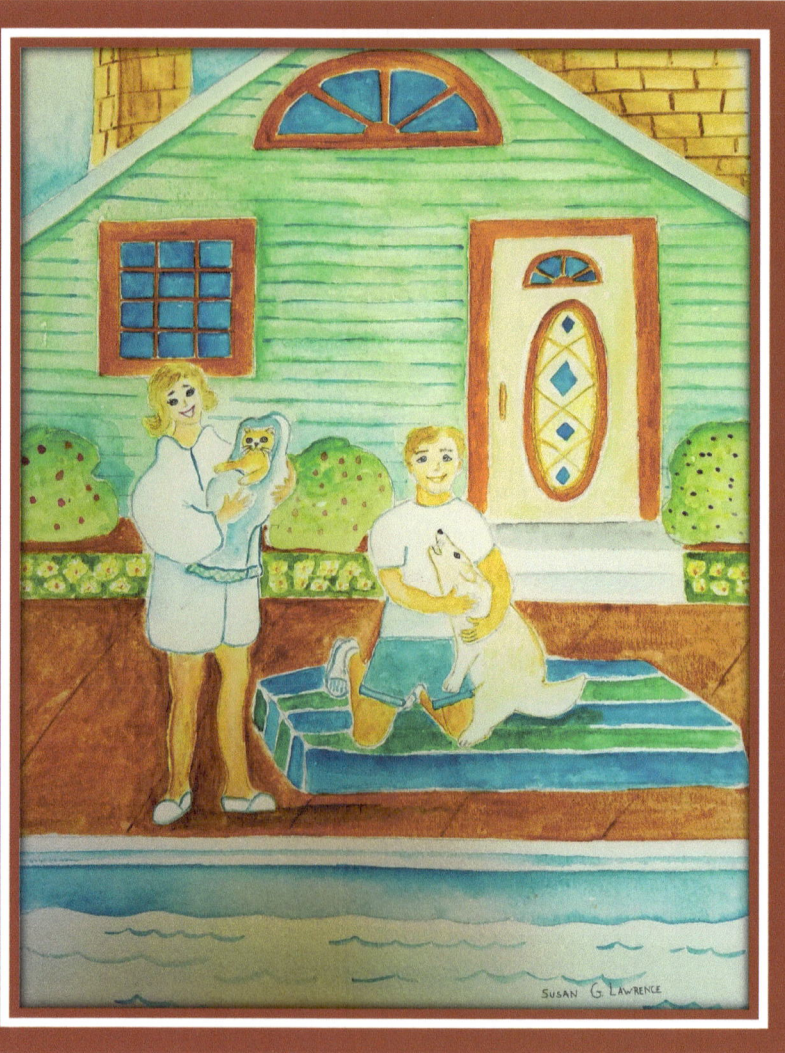

The Cat Swimmer

I was so hot and they
   were all in the pool
The dog, my dad and mother
   to all stay cool
But me a cat, they said
   No, he can't swim
So I dove in out of anger
   or maybe just a whim
But I started to paddle clear
   across to the other side
They laughed, they roared, they
   knew I had pride
Mom took me in her arms and
   wrapped me in a warm towel
I suddenly became the most respected
   while our pooch began to howl
But it proved I could be amazing
   like some of the bigger cats
They just thought I knew how to
   scare mice or chase pesty rats

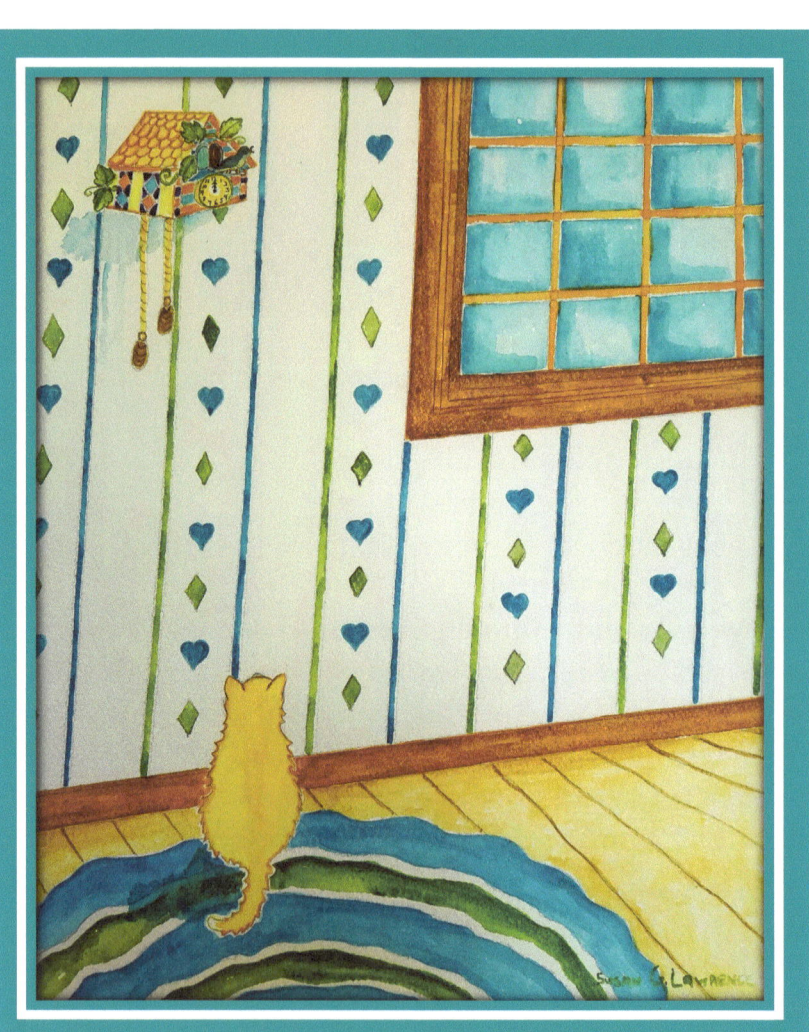

The Clock Cuckoo

I'm looking at that clock
   as I sit before the noon hour
And wait for that little bird to come
   out and shout with songful power
That small creature cannot be real
   I've never seen one like it before
But it amazes me how he is on time
   because I've kept perfect score
Even though I'm an agile cat
   he's not the least bit afraid
With his decorated house and music
   he knows he has it made
I know I can't climb up there
   the walls are really too steep
I guess we can exist together
   because it's time I got a little sleep

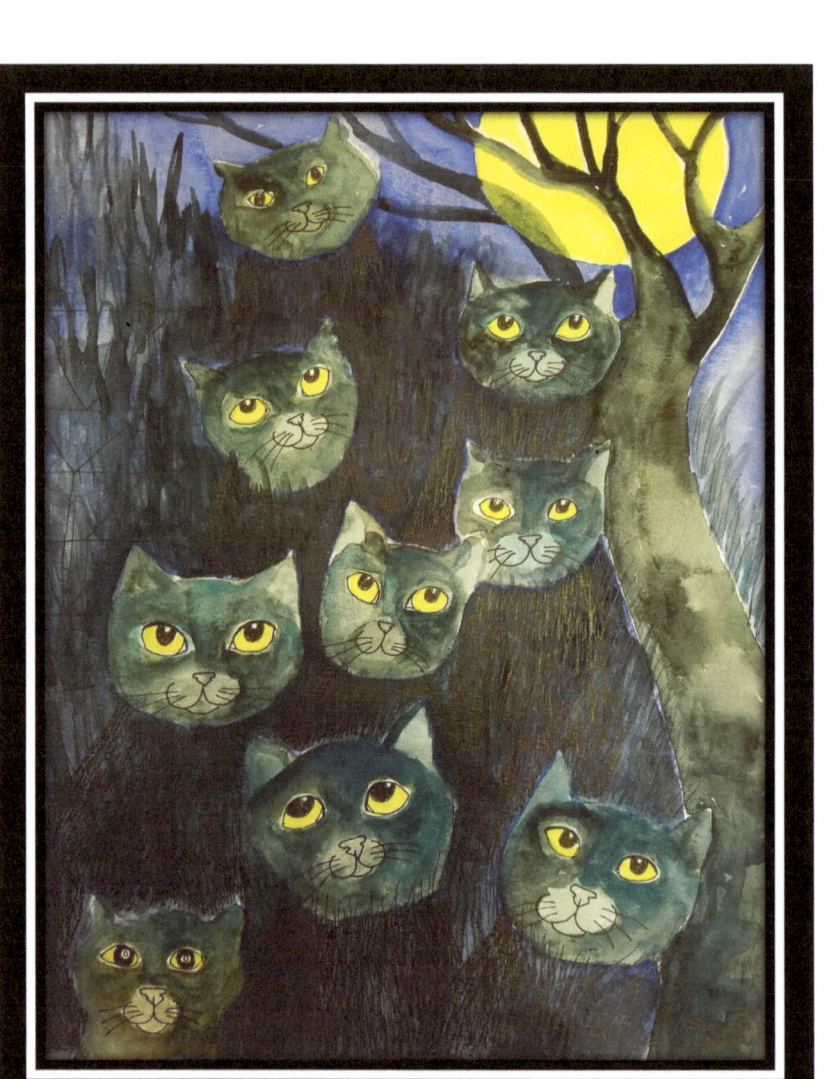

Cat Eyes in the Night

Walking through the angel cat alley
  we see cat eyes in the night
Some hidden under an old table, the
  others out in the moonlight
We thought they would talk to us
  but we weren't very sure
There were only cat eyes in the night
  surrounded by hidden fur
And standing alone by a tree was
  one who was wise and shy
We could see her a little better because
  she came closer when we asked why
In a quiet way do the eyes here say
  friendship is something you disallow
She said the cats here know just
  as your green eyes glow
It's the key to warm hearts somehow

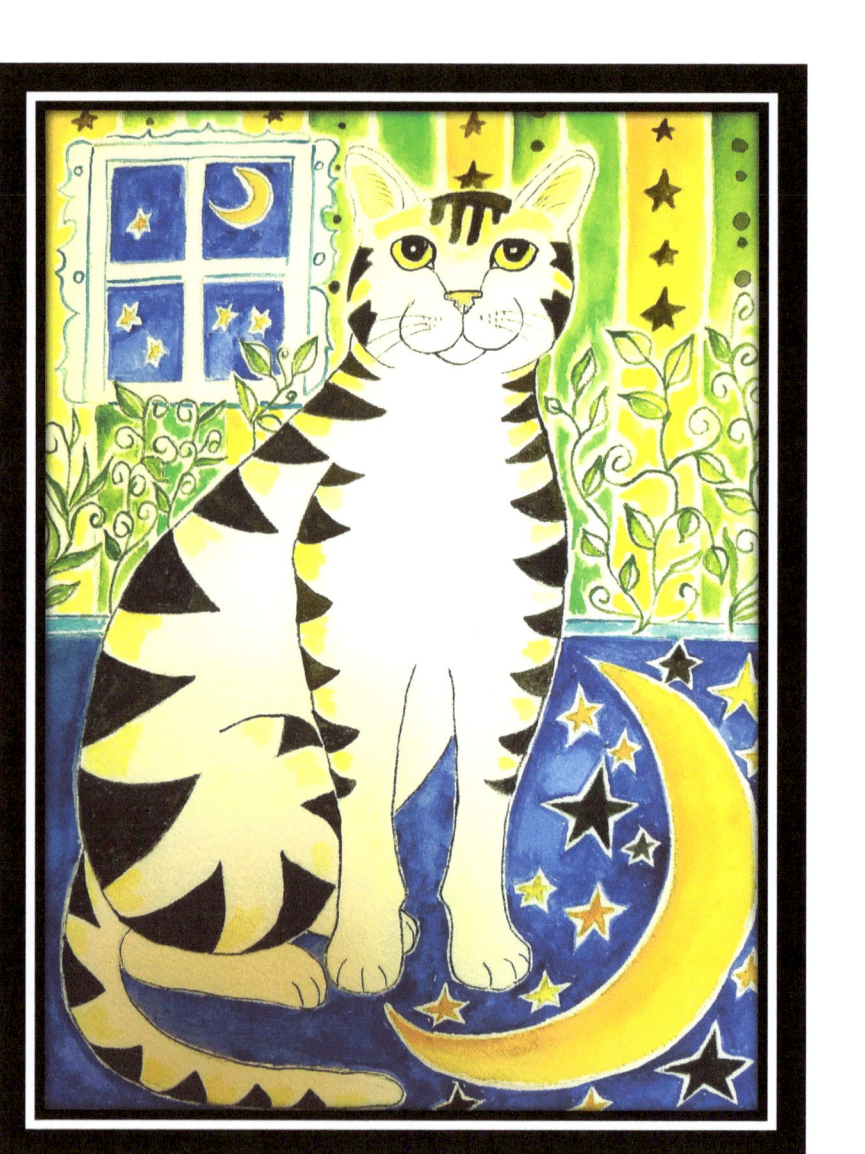

The Witch and the Cat

They called her a witch, and
  she always knew
They thought she produced
  magic in a secret stew
But she was my owner and
  she was very kind
She was creative and like me
  had a curious mind
It was always thoughtful how
  she complimented me
And always took care of everything
  she loved me for free
She was not evil or bad
  or anything like that
She just had a place where she
  thought, focused and sat
It was the creator who she
  knew came first
She was good to me, and I
  never felt cursed

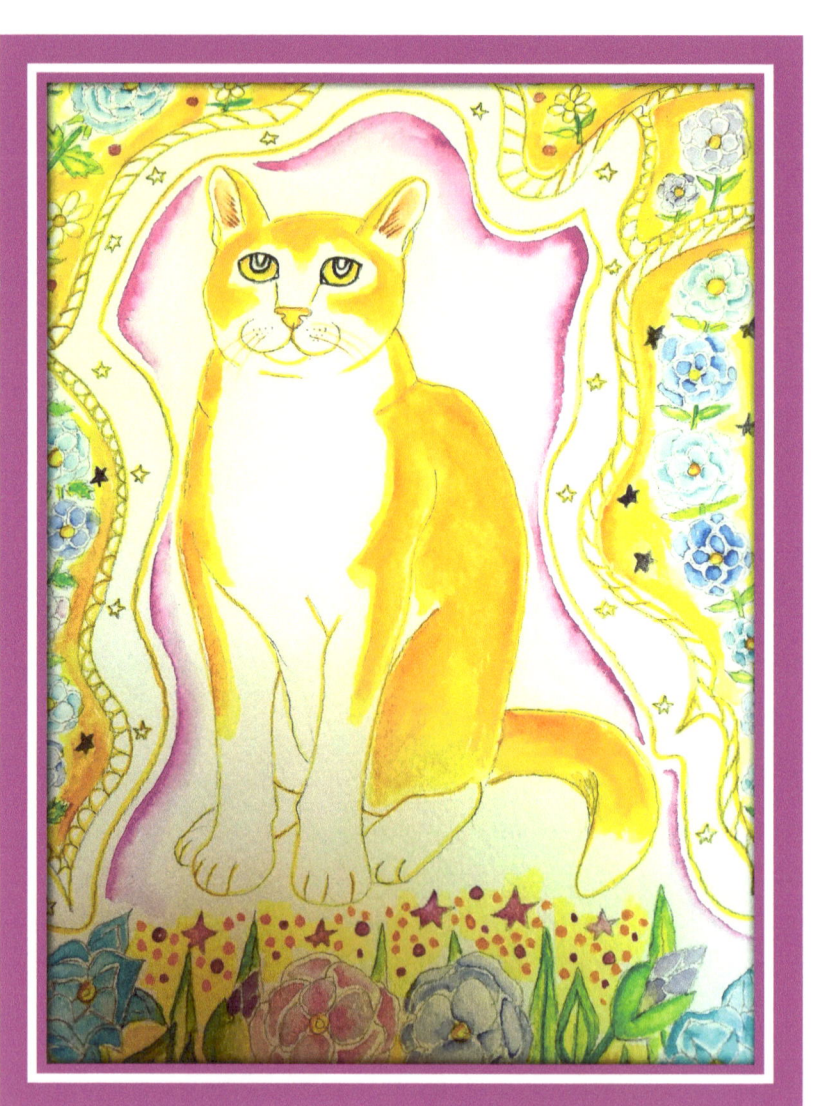

Home

This is my enchanted garden of
   pastel flowers and perennial plants
Sitting upon this antiquated porch
   I'm passing through into a trance
The fragrant aroma is so beautiful
   I feel a gentle nudging breeze of spring
Under this blue rose trellis I can
   feel the comforts of a king
The nearby evergreen tree smells fresh
   with its scent of pine
It's to me a castle I look out of
   when curious some of the time
It's all here, my home, a haven
   of never-ending peace
I'm a cat who is loved, I'm a little
   part Siamese

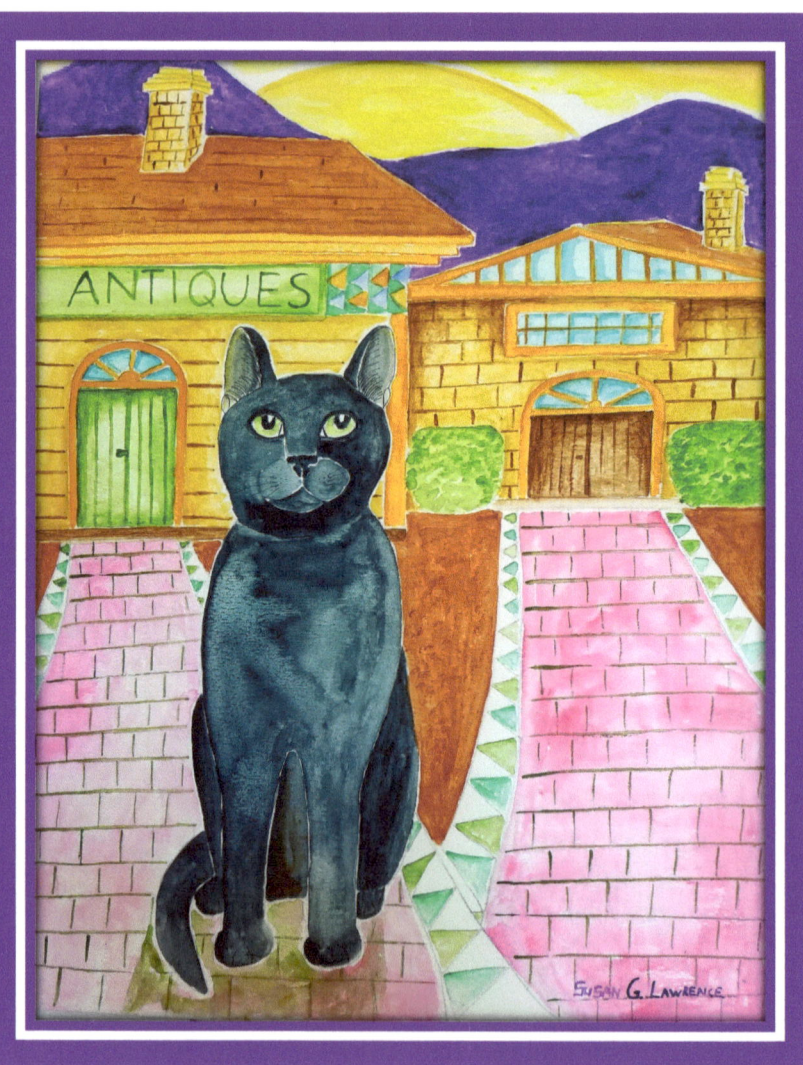

ANTIQUES

Susan G. Lawrence

The Antique Store

Here in this house of heirlooms
   I'm a Russian Blue cat with appeal
There are unusual chairs and blankets
   that are beautiful to nudge and feel
There are interesting customers who call
   me or try to get me to talk
But I like to run down this aisle way
   they call the cat walk
It may be that I'm a little shy
   and maybe a bit quiet too
But I tend to like the way old things
   are better than new
And when this elderly man drives
   me home for the early night
I know he has made my life beautiful
   his kindness is just right

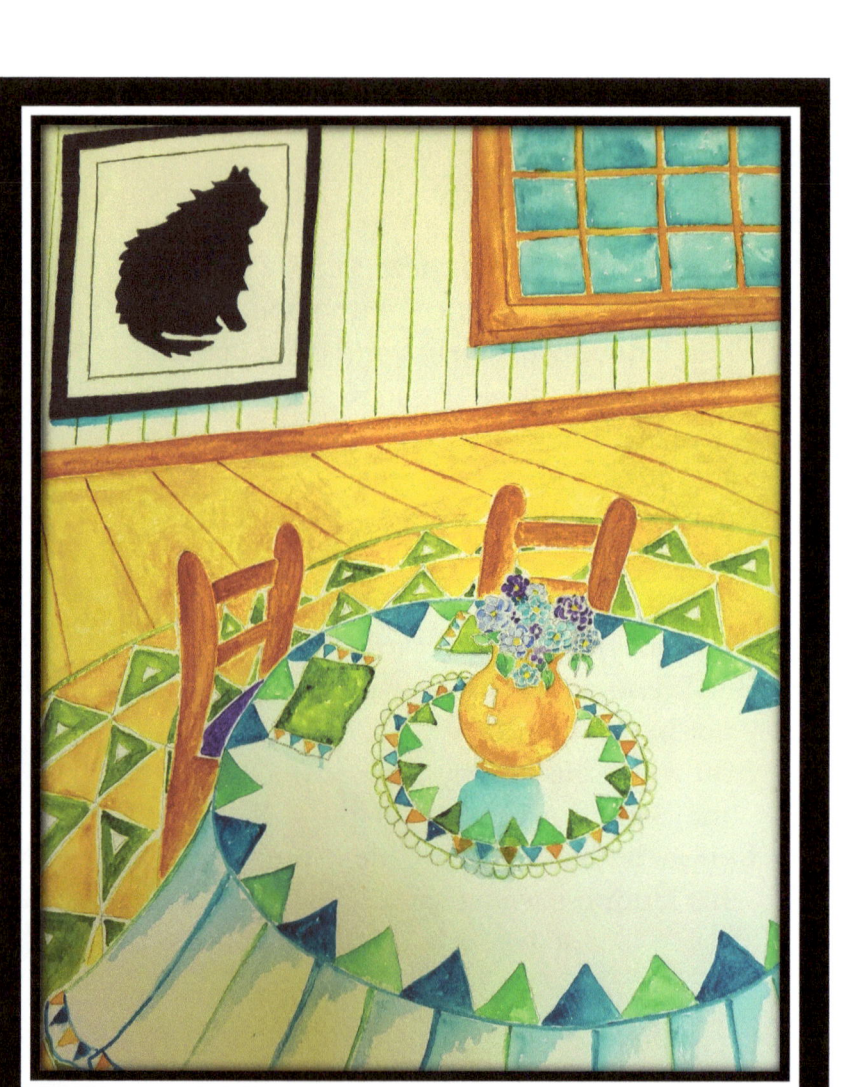

Silhouette of a Cat

A cutout outline of me
  hangs on the kitchen wall
I'm able to feel confident,
  respected and tall
In like a shadow you can
  see my wavy long fur
There is no mistaking, I'm
  a small feline for sure
A cat's features can be remembered
  forever this way
I can be comfort
  and I'm here to stay

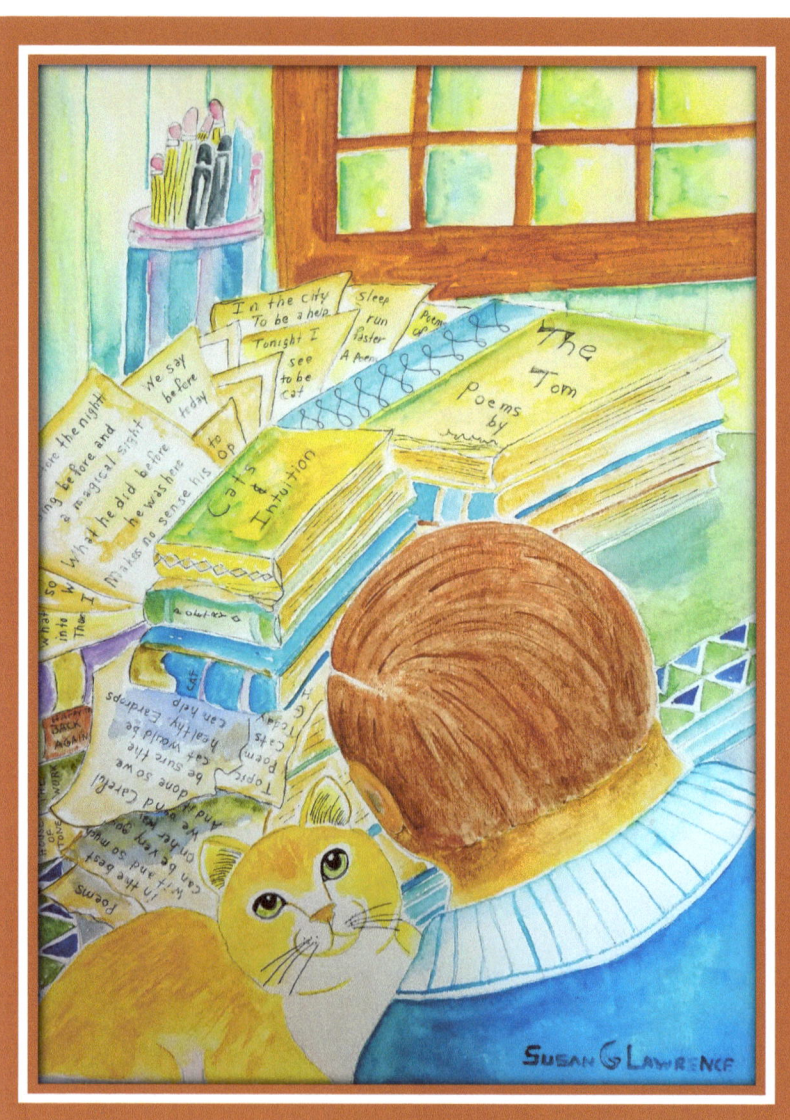

The Cat and the Poet

In his study the light from
   the morning sun streams in
I walk by and rub his legs
   he looks down at me with a grin
He is a poet so kind with a lot of
   insight for each day
It's great to be a friend of his
   he understands a better way
I lie among his papers and books,
   torn, old and new
I'm here noticing each one of his moods
   happy, wistful, and blue
And when he completes his next book
   this year again
He will finally have more time to turn
   his study into a cozy den

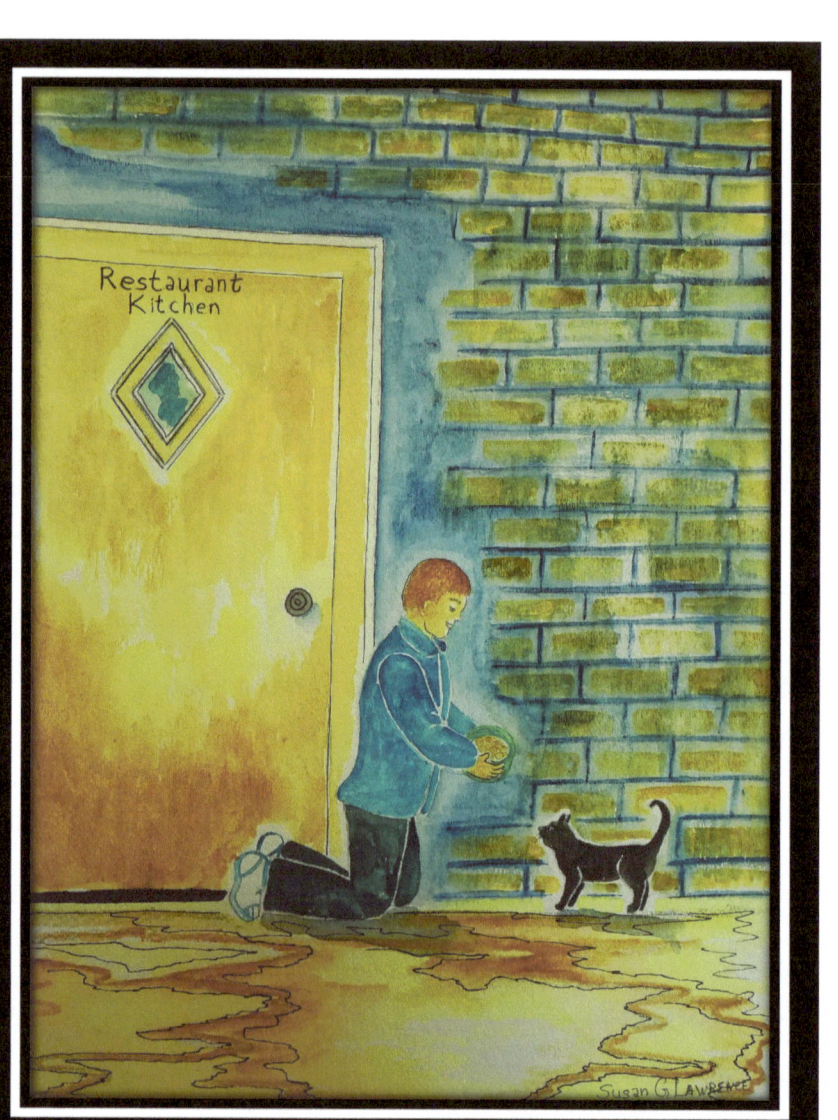

Cat of Four Paws

There is a cook who is my friend
   and knows I walk on four paws
He goes out of his way for me
   even if there are consumer laws
I climb a red maple overlooking
   the pretty outdoor café
Where different types of people pass
   through the magic brick doorway
Up here I can smell the twirling
   aroma of sautéed fish
And my partner in transgression
   comes out back with a tasty dish
So I climb down the tree to find
   the secret stone passageway
I know he always remembers
   making this another great day
And I know my true confidant
   can't be very afraid
He feels it's right to feed me
   and be a little renegade

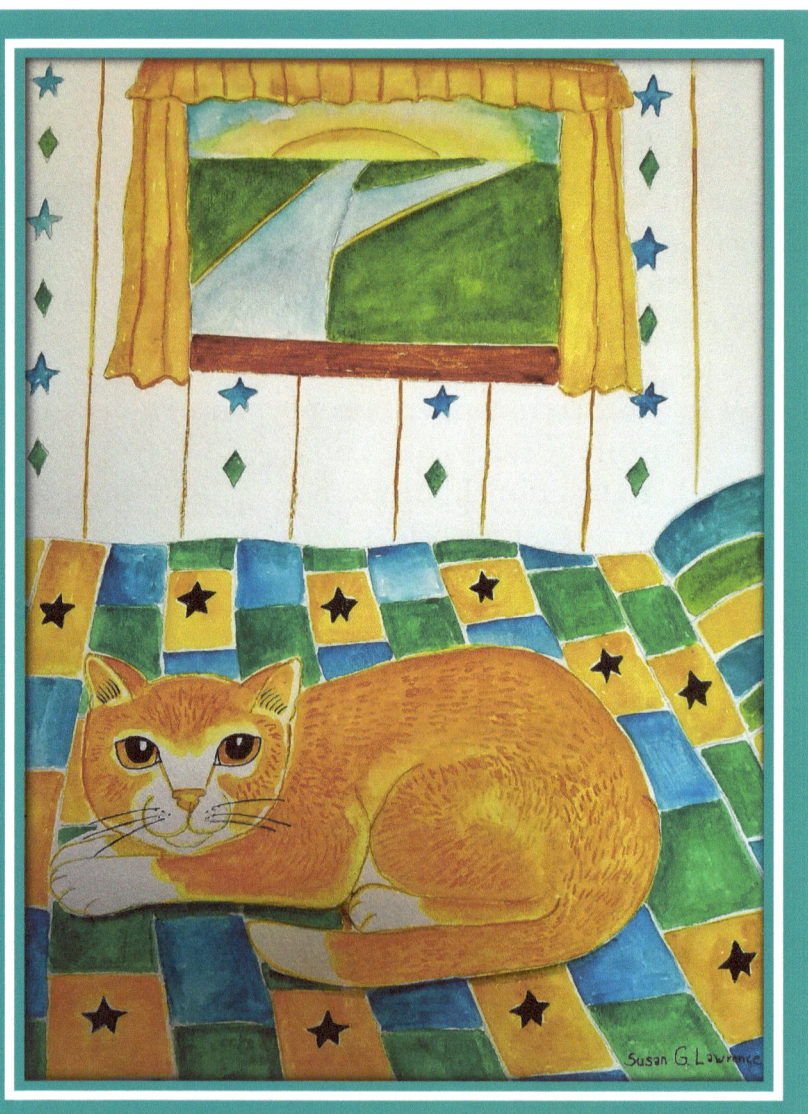

At the Crossroads

As an elder cat I've traveled
   a lot of roads
I've walked and ran on four
   legs and ten toes
And at the crossroads feeling
   I must choose a way to go
Home is where one leads where I
   can lie in the afterglow
The other is the way of ego
   and superpower
Where I can nudge and judge
   and be as tall as a tower
But as I look at the sun setting
   in the pink sky of blue hues
I know it's time to rest and review
   what I've lived through
So as I walk home to sleep in
   this countryside
I can remain here and be happy
   with a silent unspoken pride

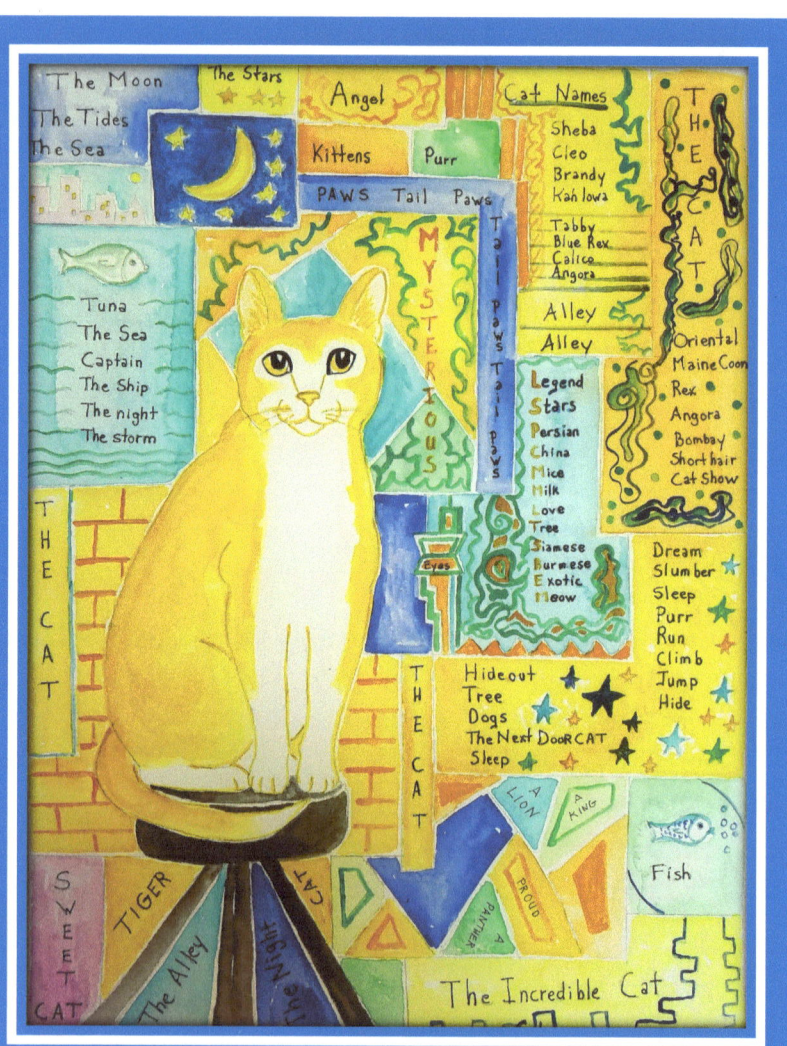

The Cat

I can be a tiger
    or a striped cat
I can leap through the air
    or be an acrobat
I can be a lion and see
    as I walk at night
I can be like a king keeping
    rodents away that fright
I can be a panther
    and outrun a snake
I can be very still and
    see my reflection in a lake
But I'm really just a little calico
    that isn't very loud
I like to be happy about myself
    I guess I'm a little proud

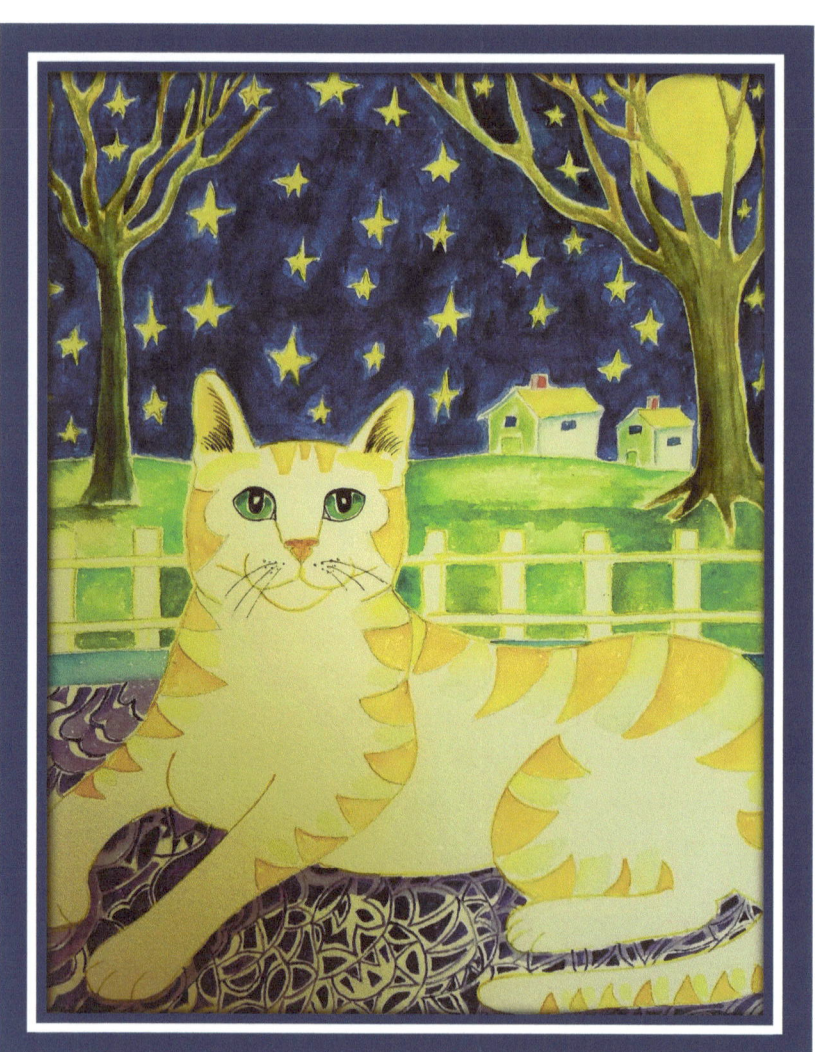

The Cat Around the Corner

In this kindly village there are
　　cats on every block
And around the corner is a good one
　　that I hope would like to talk
Now I don't know if he was ever
　　a city resident before
I just would like to go down to meet
　　him and stand by his door
So off I walked on the earth's surface
　　of dirt and pebbles around
And met him on the porch of brick
　　and cement three feet above ground
And as we purred and talked about
　　the catnip from the local feline shop
He said he thought we had been friends
　　some lives before
And frolicked in a neighborhood treetop

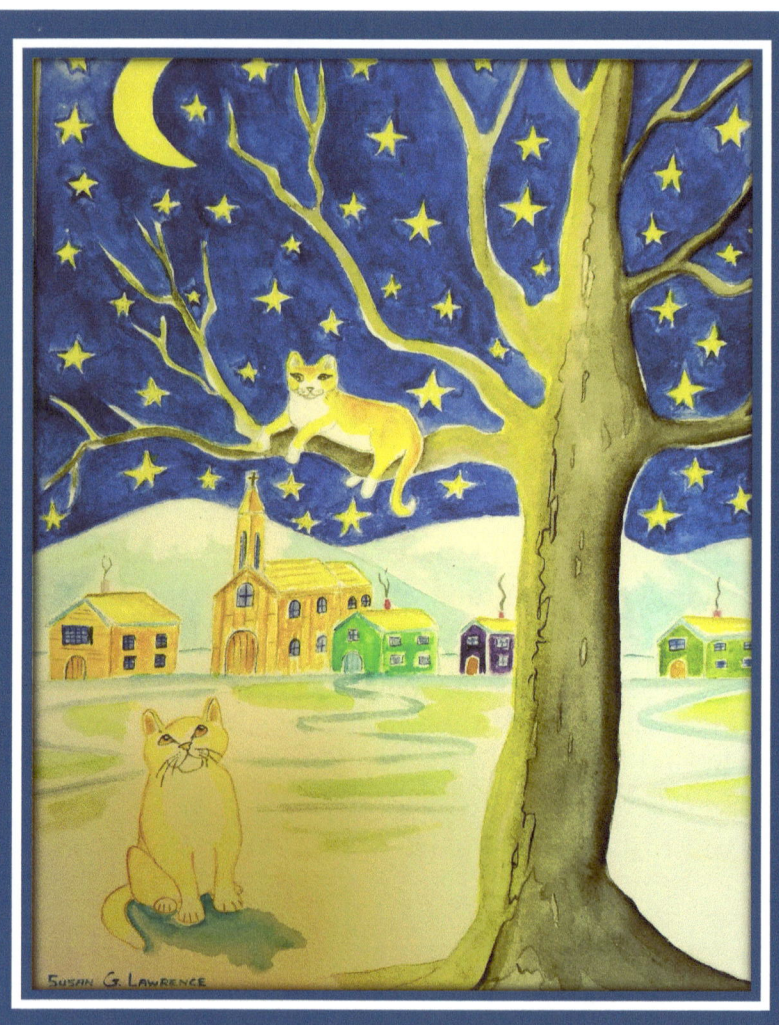

The Tom

As I sit here in this garden
   of bees, beetles and buttercups
I'm watching as Toms do the pretty
   cats in the wind, and my fur flutters up
I'm getting older and I do have more
   leisure time than when I was young
The fact that I was dashing and clever
   is not a story far-flung
There was a way to meet female felines
   somewhere back then
Somehow it's not as easy I'm more
   comfortable at home in my den
I often think back to a lovely
   face and cute curious tail
She was a tabby so beautiful
   whose home was up for sale

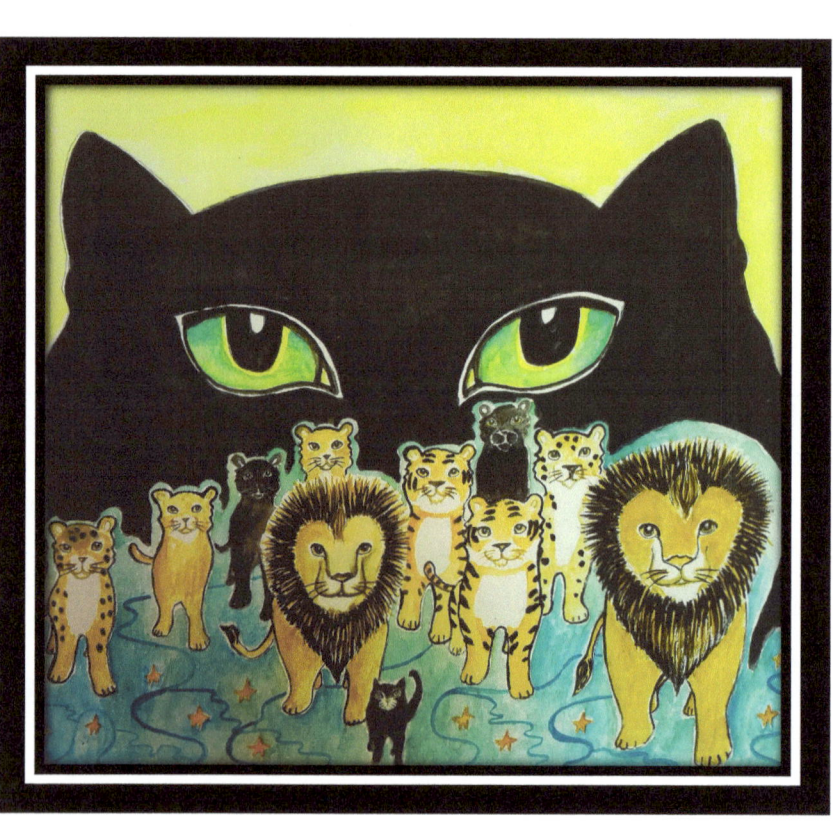

Walking with the Bigger Cats

When I gaze out the door window
   at a bright sunbeam sent down
This light hits my eyes and my mind
   hears a roaring sound
And in this dreamlike state, I'm
   walking with the bigger cats
Tigers and lions and jaguars
   of the feline aristocrat
In this imaginary place they don't
   mind that I'm so small
Because this must be a spirit world
   where you're considered just as tall
And as we walk here we are all
   family and special friends
In this creation of peace there is
   nothing we can't transcend
My spirit is uplifted by the gentle way
   these cats are so warm and tender
I know this must be a unique glimpse
   of heaven, shown to me by an angelic
   dream sender